The Angel Babies.XV. .ONE.

~*~

Clive Alando Taylor

authorHOUSE

AuthorHouse™ UK
1663 Liberty Drive
Bloomington, IN 47403 USA
www.authorhouse.co.uk
Phone: 0800 047 8203 (Domestic TFN)
+44 1908 723714 (International)

Published by AuthorHouse 10/08/2019

ISBN: 978-1-7283-9446-6 (sc)
ISBN: 978-1-7283-9445-9 (e)

Print information available on the last page.

*Any people depicted in stock imagery provided by Getty Images are models,
and such images are being used for illustrative purposes only.
Certain stock imagery © Getty Images.*

This book is printed on acid-free paper.

Angelus Domini .ONE.

INSPIRIT * ASPIRE * ESPRIT * INSPIRE

Because of the things that have first become proclaimed within the spirit, and then translated in the soul, in order for the body to then become alive and responsive or to aspire, or to be inspired, if only then for the body to become a vessel, or a catalyst, or indeed an instrument of will, with which first the living spirit that gave life to it, along with the merits and the meaning of life, and the instruction and the interpretation of life, is simply to understand that the relationship between the spirit and the soul, are also the one living embodiment with which all things are one, and become connected and interwoven by creating, or causing what we can come to call, or refer to as the essence, or the cradle, or the fabric of life, which is in itself part physical and part spirit.

And so it is, that we are all brought in being, along with this primordial and spiritual birth, and along with this the presence or the origins of the spirit, which is also the fabric and the nurturer of the soul with which the body can be formed, albeit that by human standards, this act of nature however natural, can now take place through the act of procreation or consummation, and so it is with regard to this living spirit that we are also upon our natural and physical birth, given a name and a number, inasmuch that we represent, or become identified by a color, or upon our created formation and distinction of identity, we become recognized by our individuality.

But concerning the Angels, it has always been of an interest to me how their very conception, or existence, or origin from nature and imagination, could have become formed and brought into being, as overtime I have heard several stories of how with the event of the first creation of man, that upon this event, that all the Angels were made to accept and to serve in God's creation of man, and that man was permitted to give command to these Angels in the event of his life, and the trials of his life which were to be mastered, but within this godly decree and narrative, we also see that there was all but one Angel that either disagreed or disapproved with, not only the creation of man, but also with the formation of this covenant between God and man, and that all but one Angel was Satan, who was somewhat displeased with God's creation of man, and in by doing so would not succumb or show respect or demonstrate servility or humility toward man or mankind.

As overtime it was also revealed to me, that with the creation of the Angels, that it was also much to their advantage as it was to ours, for the Angels themselves to adhere to this role and to serve in the best interest of man's endeavors upon the face of the earth, as long as man himself could demonstrate and become of a will and a nature to practice his faith with a spirit, and a soul, and a body that would become attuned to a godly or godlike nature, and in by doing so, and in by believing so, that all of his needs would be met with accordingly.

And so this perspective brings me to question my own faith and ideas about the concept and the ideology of Angels, insomuch so that I needed to address and to explore my own minds revelation, and to investigate that which I was told or at least that which I thought I knew concerning the Angels along with the juxtaposition that if Satan along with those Angels opposed to serving God's creation of man, and of those that did indeed seek to serve and to favor God's creation and to meet with the merits, and the dreams, and the aspirations of man, that could indeed cause us all to be at the mercy and the subjection of an externally influential and internal spiritual struggle or spiritual warfare, not only with ourselves, but also with our primordial and spiritual identity.

And also because of our own conceptual reasoning and comprehension beyond this event, is that we almost find ourselves astonished into believing that this idea of rights over our mortal souls or being, must have begun or started long ago, or at least long before any of us were even souls inhabiting our physical bodies here as a living presence upon the face of the earth, and such is this constructed dilemma behind our beliefs or identities, or the fact that the names, or the numbers that we have all been given, or that have at least become assigned to us, is simply because of the fact that we have all been born into the physical world.

As even I in my attempts, to try to come to terms with the very idea of how nature and creation could allow so many of us to question this reason of totality, if only for me to present to you the story of the Angel Babies, if only to understand, or to restore if your faith along with mine, back into the realms of mankind and humanity, as I have also come to reflect in my own approach and understanding of this narrative between God and Satan and the Angels, that also in recognizing that they all have the power to influence and to subject us to, as well as to direct mankind and humanity, either to our best or worst possibilities, if only then to challenge our primordial spiritual origin within the confines of our own lifestyles, and practices and beliefs, as if in our own efforts and practices that we are all each and every one of us, in subjection or at least examples and products of both good and bad influences.

Which is also why, that in our spiritual nature, that we often call out to these heavenly and external Angelic forces to approach us, and to heal us, and to bless us spiritually, which is, or has to be made to become a necessity, especially when there is a humane need for us to call out for the assistance, and the welfare, and the benefit of our own souls, and our own bodies to be aided or administered too, or indeed for the proper gifts to be bestowed upon us, to empower us in such a way, that we can receive guidance and make affirmations through the proper will and conduct of a satisfactory lesson learnt albeit through this practical application and understanding, if only to attain spiritual and fruitful lives.

As it is simply by recognizing that we are, or at some point or another in our lives, have always somewhat been open, or subject to the interpretations of spiritual warfare by reason of definition, in that Satan's interpretation of creation is something somewhat of contempt, in that God should do away with, or even destroy creation, but as much as Satan can only prove to tempt, or to provoke God into this reckoning, it is only simply by inadvertently influencing the concepts, or the ideologies of man, that of which whom God has also created to be creators, that man through his trials of life could also be deemed to be seen in Satan's view, that somehow God had failed in this act of creation, and that Satan who is also just an Angel, could somehow convince God of ending creation, as Satan himself cannot, nor does not possess the power to stop or to end creation, which of course is only in the hands of the creator.

And so this brings me back to the Angels, and of those that are in favor of either serving, or saving mankind from his own end and destruction, albeit that we are caught up in a primordial spiritual fight, that we are all engaged in, or by reason of definition born into, and so it is only by our choices that we ultimately pay for our sacrifice, or believe in our rights to life, inasmuch that we are all lifted up to our greatest effort or design, if we can learn to demonstrate and to accept our humanity in a way that regards and reflects our greater desire or need, to be something more than what we choose to believe is only in the hands of God the creator or indeed a spirit in the sky.

Angelus Domini. XV.

Time is neither here or there, it is a time in between time as it is the beginning and yet the end of time. This is a story of the Alpha and the Omega, the first and the last, and yet as we enter into this revelation, we begin to witness the birth of the Angel Babies a time of heavenly conception when dying Angels gave birth to Angelic children who were born to represent the order of the new world. The names of these Angel Babies remained unknown but they carried the Seal of their fathers written on their foreheads, and in all it totalled one hundred and forty four thousand Angels and this is the story of one of them.

~*~

Angelus Domini

INSPIRIT * ASPIRE * ESPRIT * INSPIRE

.ONE.XV.

~*~

Angelus E'Diurnāl

INSPIRIT * ASPIRE * ESPRIT * INSPIRE

.ONE..XV.

Angelus Domini One

Uck-Han-Dudullud, The first voice, and the only sound which I heard was like a (Trumpet!) and in coming forth from out of the reddish mist, where once upon the darkness that was too unbearable had begun to lift marking the beginnings of a new dawn and a new star arising, *Angelus E' Diurnāl*, as you have beckoned me to respond, then so in kind I shall duly do so, for the world is ravaged with every kind of plague and disaster after it, and yet all is soon to be banished and expelled at will, if it shall be deemed so, by he that removes the wicked pillars that have stood for a time in all eternity, towards fulfilling the scriptures and prophetic promises of the Earth now laid bare and barren before me, for permit me to speak as a witness, that I did not have any more befitting words to utter or speak, except that which has gone out before me, in saying that worth is the lamb that has removed the last seal, for even before the ages had begun, it was for this reason that the One would come forth from out of the nothingness in order to restore the balance and fullness thereof, except that none should, or could not know or solve why, in bearing and having full authority over all things both now and forevermore *Dudullud-Uck-Han*

Uck-Han-Dudullud, Permit me to speak of only what is probable, set against the impossible, for the Earth is a witness to itself, for that which has taken place across the ages, and yet every seed which has sprung forth from her bosom was hewn down, and for anything that was committed against her, even unto the latter days of this imminent age, as nothing was left undone, and yet everything was to be said of her, lest we should forget, the why and wherefore, that time itself has become reset, to mark the beginning of the end, and the beginning of the beginning itself, for where else are these men of god, and these sages of prophets, and these martyrs of faith and these saints of virtue now, when measured up against those of whom had spilt such innocent blood, shed for the causation of seven deadly sins, now to be transcended by seven virtues, as I can only speak of the unspeakable *Dudullud-Uck-Han.*

Uck-Han-Dudullud For now the world has fallen empty and silent, if only for the preparedness of its' renewal and rejuvenation, revival and restoration, as I saw a new earth and a new heaven begin to unfold and manifest, as the entire household bore witness to the creator of the first heavens, beginning to invent, and to compose, to modify and enhance, and tp reanimate and reenact, and to cause motion and movement, and to strike against the seeds of nature, to cultivate and nurture it, and to cause growth to excite it, and to ignite and carve out in attendance to it, and to cause all manner of influences against the birds of the wind, and the fishes teeming together in the waters, and the wildlife, and all the manner of creatures that were made to gather and flock together, were also commanded in their silences, to utter all manner of sounds, in giving glory to the One, *Dudullud-Uck-Han.*

Uck-Han-Dudullud Even the Earth herself, was caused to open up the womb of her belly, in sustaining herself o give birth to the newness of her creation, as all that was done, and undone, was now to be made whole and complete in his sight, for he that hath said 'I am the light of this world, and the world is in me, as you are also of the world, and the world is also inside of you" had arisen and awoken from the dreams of the dream world, and fulfilled the spirits of the spirit world, and solved the mystery of mysteries, and was now readily prepared to set down, and bring about a kingdom that would fulfill the Deen of Jannah, so that the Heavens could be set apart like a glorified Gemstone set within the heart of the entire universe *Dudullud-Uck-Han.*

Uck-Han-Dudullud s they did not know his name, until his name was called, as it was upon hearing this name, that they knew who he was and what he was instructed to do, to make a Covenant from the beginning of time, until the end of days, and so it was that as he appeared to them, that they were not made to fall down in worship but made to stand up in righteousness, and as they were made to receive him in kind, and then thereafter they did hear him in saying, *Uck-Han-Dudullud,* 'the coming of a new age is upon us, and yet untoward your allegiances, it shall agitate one, and incense the other, for even those of you who have been called and brought before to witness the secrets of the sacred heart, set against the tale of this the holy grail, and the infinite Sum of all eternity to open up the heavenly gates, and to contemplate, upon all that lives and breathes, as a chosen One is deemed elected and worthy, to overcome Diablo and all his grand mastery of conjuring wizards and sorcery, distorting reality, but do not be afraid of dragons and serpents, as one Crucified and brought back to life through the resurrection, as One redeems, to fulfill your Deen, upon these roads to Jannah, as your swords are now turned into words of inquiry and examination, in knowing now, that you ablution has given you over to the will of your submission.

'For did not the broadest shoulders, bear the heaviest load, and yet it was never a burden to my soul concerning the broadest churches both outside and within, for it is now newly formed as a another place, where all these things shall take place and shape to begin, for what else remains and who shall stay, now that we see the end of days, set against the sounds of war, knowing that the beast is drumming preparing for my coming, and yet only love could say it true, for who else has done thus much for you, or do you only believe in the things you see, as you try to solve these mystery's of truth, unless I should take you back to another place where the final act was committed, for everything has changed, to now know that it was not in vain, and so take this seed from me and plant it now wherever you may stand, as it is for all these dreams to come true and prevail and yet cannot succeed before I fail, as nothing else can explain, except that the wind is calling my name, and yet have not all these things come to pass, and of those who were summonsed even unto death, are given over to a new body, and a new mind, and a new heart, and a new soul, and does now the spirit dwell there within you'.

Someone Said, 'when will you come, and who will you save, will it be me, am I worth it today, is there something else more important to see, who will you take and who will you leave, as I've tried to forgive and never forsake, and I've tried to be strong when I was ready to break, I've tried to hold on, and tried to believe, and I've tried to love you, when you was loving me, so why would you breathe your breath into these broken bones, to suffer a lifetime of heartache and pain, as it is something I do not wish to endure again, and now that you've come, why should we go back just to see everything start to break and crack, was it not enough to see you on the Cross and realize everything was lost' 'I know that you are afraid to live again, but this is not how the story ends, as it will not be as it was before, and much unlike the day that you were born'.

'Once we had fallen at your feet, would you not now allow us this time just to sleep, have we not already succumb and seen what it means to be young, as for now, are we not over and done with, have we not yet come to the end of the road, was not being good just not good enough, does it take much more than we've ever known, just like the serpent Ouroborus, are we forever destined to shed our skin only to consume our clothes, and where shall we go at the end of time, if only to fall at your feet once more, in exposing our souls through timeless expressions of prayer and invocations that once defeated us' 'Wake up now, for you are all still asleep, even now as you walk alone, did not my mercy come to conquer one and all, and did you not once agree that we cannot live by bread alone, and yet be reminded of the vulgar vile things that were once spoken of when you were as the empty vessel, and did I not commit the will to purge the soul, restoring it, to all to its' cleanliness, and yet for all of the good things ever said, did you not watch and witness a soul curl up and die, in all preparedness, waiting for such spirits to rise up again, and do you no longer see, that this need of the past to repeat in endless repetition is no more, as you, who no longer need to choose or decide, to live and then lose your life all over again, can you not see that the truth is bearing fruit, providing us with more than hope beyond these circles of infinity, for love is the root by which all are measured'.

Uck-Han-Dudullud, in addressing the poor in spirit and those of whom were meek, and also those whom had mourned and also those whom had hungered and thirsted, and of those whom were merciful and pure in heart, and also those of whom were peacemakers, and those of whom were also persecuted and reviled against, as they had now come to know their comforter standing within the midst of their righteousness, as they were now filled with the spirit and readily prepared to receive this, their inheritance of the earth, as it was through his mercy that the children of God did see God in the kingdom of heaven, and began to gladly rejoice exceedingly for his sake in acknowledging his saying thus Dudullud-Uck-Han, 'therefore through the fulfillment of these beatitudes, you are found to be worthy, and i am happy and abundantly blessed and satisfied with you, as I am forever with you always, and everywhere throughout the ages of all time'.

'Fear not, for you surely did not die, but instead were brought right back to your senses, as this kingdoms I now proclaim, can only but rise again, in observing these the last days and the five pillars, as within the circle which is now complete, as you now solidly pound upon your heart as you beat your chest, whereupon once you covered me with your anointing, while serpents were trodden down by my feet, and even the animals of my kingdom did testify upon giving their accounting, and yet I did only see to take charge to accept my own truth in the presence of the Father and the Holy Ghost, even when everything was crashing down, and yet did I not ascend to the humble abode of the spirits way above the sky, and yet those of little faith, who knew not how they were saved, or how far they had strayed from the things they believed were done in my name, and not that of your father, or that of my father, but that of our father, for thou art in heaven upon this day, and yet in turning the pages and shifting through the ages, and those seeking after me, watching and waiting for change in all of its' phases, and in finding out the truth, which might not have been so amazing from revelation to revelation, except that it is through me that all thing are now pronounced to come forth and begin again upon the end of the ages, surely I come quickly'.

Uck-Han-Dudullud As the entirety of the multitudes gathered themselves together, not only to hear but to receive the significance of the time immemorial, that had now come to fill their empty cup of their vessels with new life, empowered with the holy spirit, and now to be fulfilled by an unbreakable bond of this new heaven, as each and every one of them had come to acknowledge the reality and the passing of an old age, as it was now that the book of the never ending ages was finally opened by *Angelus pablo establo estebhan augustus diablo*, the immortal one, keeper of the unwritten laws *Dudullud-Uck-Han.*

Angelus Pablo

321

1 Hark! the herald angels sing
glory to the new-born King;
peace on earth and mercy mild,
God and sinners reconciled!
Joyful all you nations rise,
join the triumph of the skies;
with the angelic host proclaim,
'Christ is born in Bethlehem':
Hark! the herald angels sing
glory to the new-born King.

highest heaven adore

Lord;

The Immortal One

Keeper Of The Unwritten Laws

A Declaration of Heaven is to recognize that the words and the books that are written of Men & Women in the most highest and natural order of our worldly civilizations, is one that brings about, or is of both an inspirational and aspiring revelation and teaching, that have been brought to us, to realize that the position of authority and the valuable authenticity born of our insights, as to what these words and books in their many varied forms, and in all their practical and tangible examples and explanations, can really define, or teach us in their application and meaning, to help us to really see as to what they can account for, or lead us towards in their teaching, and availability and readiness to enhance, and to influence us in their balance and impact upon our lives.

As often enough we all seek to discredit and to sometimes challenge, or even adhere to, or to undermine and question the very principle core of asking or pursuing, what is a path to the potentiality of a truth recognized, and what comes forth from such a truth of paramount importance and dedication and devotion, if only for it to be recognized and revealed to us upon our examination of it, along with the principle teaching and motives behind such books and literature and manuscripts, as to whether such influential material does indeed come to be initially constituted and subscribed to and purposely written by a hand that is governed by, and initially upon instruction, that which is of an open or devoted mind, that has become attuned or ordained by that of a divine nature.

As such are the merits of our activities in detecting that we are all aligned through faith and understanding, to be both accurate and comprehensive in its' intermittent message of guidance and intent, if only for us all to become easily transcendental and reflective, and effectively empowered upon the instrumental bearing of our spiritual inclinations towards life, and so the verity of this verification, is upon us in being both responsive and submissive to the sub-truth, and the real reality of the underlying matter, to belong to that which is causing, and to that which is influencing the empowered spirit behind the fundamental idea, and the primal origin of such life sustaining and affirming properties locked and embedded within the nature of this declaration.

A Declaration of Heaven is made and achieved, when the medium of our ability to understand and comprehend, that through our journeying and with our acceptance, that we in the World, with all its natural resources, which has always maintained and sustained us as a Race & a People, in our every need and development to survive as a Race & a People, in realizing and recognizing that not all is as it could or should be, in us, perfecting ourselves as a creation upon the face of the World.

A Declaration of Heaven, is for each and every freedom to be recognized and realized in knowing that we have evolved within our constructs of idealism and ideas, out of struggles and revolutions, to begin to advance in tackling and changing the religious and political landscape structured within our beliefs and ideologies, if only to begin to deal with, and to come to terms with, the impact reality of such realities, like World poverty, and Universal relationships, and Ecological and Environmental issues, that have often held us back from make such declarations, in bringing together the underlying uniformity, that we as Human beings must face within the future of our own growth and long lasting development as a Race & a People upon the face of the Planet.

A Declaration of Heaven is also necessary in knowing, that in spite of our indifferences, and choice of lifestyles, that somehow we all have a common place, and a unifying common relationship within the Union of Humankind & Humanity, in realizing, that unless we make such concerted efforts to make such a declaration of a heaven pertaining to be, that what we shall see overtime, is that we shall cease to arrive at a point in time, when we, with all our knowledge and power of understanding cannot find it in our hearts to submit ourselves to find the resolute choice of answers, that could lead us to begin to readdress these Worldly challenges that affect us all, as we must begin to enlighten ourselves and practice an ethical and principled act of motives, in aspiring where we can, to find the common thread, that is our unifying and common interests, that relate to us all, despite where we live, or what we can begin to achieve to overcome against such Global phenomena.

A Declaration of Heaven is also a means of us coming to terms with the growth and the maintenance in the Global race to save our planet and ourselves, by positively working together to solve all of our man made problems, as such are the effects that we now all too often see and witness in such calamities, as Climate change, and so we must also seek to overcome and develop, and bring resolve to such external factors, as well as deal with other internal affairs and factors in finding agreements that can no longer set us up as separate Nations in the Global race to be apart from one another, as such issues as Race & Gender, Beliefs & Politics affect us all, and so we must learn to move toward, and create a basis for understanding, acceptance, and tolerance, and compassion on a universal scale.

A Declaration of Heaven is for every individual to look at Him or Herself as the first and initial point of interest, that everything begins and ends with us as individuals, by contributing and playing a role with the wider and broader context, and in being aware of the choices and the decisions that we make, and that are laid out in front of us, can impact and have a lasting effect on us all, but more especially on a positive note, if we are to progress systematically, so as to work towards fulfilling our integral role of importance, not only to our selves, but also to what is the best choice of effort and regard for each other as a Race & a People, and for what we have and can achieve within the framework of progress toward creating what is for the betterment of our Deliverance, in the name of Salvation, Humanity, Love & Peace, then we must endeavor to do so.

A Declaration of Heaven is the view and the vision of Humanity and that of Mankind, to begin reconciling ourselves back to, and within the realms of Dignity & Respect & Happiness in creating stability not only as a Race & a People but also upon the face of the Planet, but also in knowing that if we cannot accept and tolerate one another beyond these ideas of formality, then we would most certainly jeopardize each and every one of these unique and special relationships of trust and bond in our walk and way of life, as well as putting the importance of our Planet at risk, and so the World as we know is put in danger, as we all need to correspondingly accept, that this is of the highest importance, in that we need to live, and to survive as such relationships need to be maintained and reaffirmed and reminded again and again that we are all interdependent upon each other's successes, and as for each and every person to become naturally and automatically included as individuals, in being included in subscribing to, and learning to find ways with which to engage with one another, in order to achieve and to have a shared and common interest, and for us to be presented with the choices of belonging to, and to stand alongside with, His or Her fellow Man or Woman.

A Declaration of Heaven means that Wars can no longer be the solution to controlling, or influencing, or to be used as the tool to threaten or to lead us to the destructive outcomes of such crimes against Humanity like Genocide, especially as the rest of the World looks on to watch in the name of such detached horror and shame, as this had always been our unforgiveable way, and our unforgettable history to date, but as for when we as individual make such declarations of heaven, it is simply to say because we have finally become enlightened and evolved enough to finally and completely understand, why we must make such statements a positive affirmation and statement in our lives from here on in, for if we do not make such life affirmative statements, then inadvertently, we are destroying ourselves, and everything, and everyone including our Planet, and for no other reason, other than we simply do not care about the outcome of our actions, as a Race and People upon the face of the Planet.

A Declaration of Heaven is made, when we begin to realize that we have always addressed the same problems in the same way, and the outcome to that problem has always been the same outcome, however the arising problems have not always been dealt with, and so with the effect to change the overall outcome wholeheartedly as deemed completely solved and acceptable in its entire outcome, we must search ourselves, to learn, and to endeavor to create new choices, and new opportunities, and to give new ideas and ideals a reasonable chance to take root and grow, and we must delegate to give a voice to others whom we might not recognize as being beneficial to our Global and Universal aspirations, so they too can help to influence us, in and out of our fixed decisions, and we must learn to listen, and to participate, and we must learn to change and to accept new realities, and we must seek to grow as individuals, and we must face new horizons, and begin to comprehend a new chapter in the name of this unknown future projection wherever and whenever these declarations are made.

A Declaration of Heaven is for us to be conscientiously aware, that as we learn to seek and to understand such an affirmative declaration, that it is only to positively change, or to engage in challenging our economical impact, or that of our lifestyles and our way of life, if only to somewhat address our inseparable and somewhat unique ecological relationship with that of our planet and environment, as we must become aware of our interconnectedness, as we remain yet somewhat deeply rooted, and somewhat volatile, and yet fundamentally naïve of our dependency within ourselves and upon that of our ecology.

As also within the natural laws of progression, and that of our natural evolutionary and advancing impact upon the environment, and that coupled with natures ability to change course, or to be somewhat unpredictable within its universal laws of influence upon our lives, and that which results in having a lasting impact upon us, and also upon that which is our way or choice of lifestyle and that of our livelihoods, is for us to acknowledge and to be forewarned of our own advances, of how that nature has always directly or indirectly related to us and how we go about forecasting and navigating our social activity as we go about our day to day living.

As much more than before, we have become much more aware of how our social activity, and action of intentions, which were once seen to be deemed the acceptable norm, of what we would have once taken for granted, is now being threatened in our awareness that within these predictable terms and means, that it has now become realized and dawned upon us, that as we begin to soberly realize, that this deeply rooted connection between us and the environment, does, and can have an effect upon us all in a number of significant ways, however small or gradual such irreversible and progressive these degrees and subtle factors may be in changing the landscape of our future, as we must somehow seek to change, or to at least challenge this way of life or being, in coming to terms with tackling these subtle changes that may take effect and have a resulting impact upon that of our immediate existence, and that of future events in our lives.

A Declaration of Heaven, is to simply acknowledge that Heaven on Earth has to become born and constructed by Man & Woman alike, as we in ourselves have inadvertently and directly made and created everything on Earth through the gifts and the skills and the insights and understanding that we naturally have inherently, and as we have already seen, that it is so easy for us to neglect and to destroy it, by simply creating hell on Earth, and so only we as a Race and a People, must also realize that we have the answer and the ability to create such solutions in regaining our common foresight and sensibility, so as to put our decision making into action, and to begin learning and applying the lessons of changing our approach and ideas of strategy, and set about bringing this declaration of Heaven into focus and into the very heart of our lives.

A Declaration of Heaven, is not to focus and to look upon these words with skepticism or negative doubts, or ill-intent and suspicion, or to make light trivial mockery, in denying or disproving such a declaration, for we would cause insult and emotional ruin to our own selves within the disposition of this life, and whether we choose to cast our aspersions elsewhere, in an attempt to deflect or reject the fault or lack in our ability and ourselves, is also a trait of uselessness to our devoted lesson, and so we must not seek to find fault with one another, as this is not the instruction, or message of intent if we are to find, or to follow the correct approach as to what language this declaration may afford to take, or should seemingly turn out to be, or with regards even sound like, as we are often too quick and hasty to cause affliction and persecution within our own voices of insinuating accusations, or holding each other in contempt, as attempt to analyze, and to scrutinize it's intended philosophy, causing us to miss the greater meaning behind the picture that it announces to teach us, and reveal to us, a value which is more accorded to a Universal teaching and voice of nature.

As we who have not yet found the courage to announce such declarations, are yet to be proven by the words of our own promises to uphold its integrity and being, for if one were to declare war, then naturally we all would know what lies beyond and beneath its statement and reckoning, as we have countless times already done so, and proven our voices to be heard in that one can command, and confrontation, and challenge, and dictate, as this ends to a means takes upon its' every term and medium in such matters, but if we were to think, and to choose, and to decide otherwise, then ought we not to attempt to diffuse the time bomb of our own destruction, and attempt to uncover the mysteries that are granted to us all, if we should indeed choose to make a declaration of Heaven.

A Declaration of Heaven, requires us to make positive steps towards creating an environment in both our local communities, and also one that aspires to promotes our society in a broader context to reflect upon and to inspire our relations within the international communities, and also one that promotes positive international relations, so that we can build upon a unifying consensus, in knowing that we as a Race & a People, can be both diverse and inclusive in developing relationships that translate across the Globe, and by us inviting in an openness towards everyone contributing and sharing our values, and experiences and insights, in both a safe and welcoming place, in being one that allows our atmosphere to flourish, and for us to feel free and at Liberty to come together with such understanding and unity.

A Declaration of Heaven is to understand, that you have a responsibility and duty to help, and to protect, and to serve your fellow Man & Woman, and to be responsible in your actions of doing so, whether you have a Job or not, you still have to come to terms with the reality that you still have a Job and a duty to set for yourself, to succeed in setting goals and fulfilling dreams of achievement for yourself with which to improve your life chances, and choices and skills for life. As we cannot idly sit by and expect something to come to life or fruition without us having already done something with which to put or set this reality into motion, to then present to us, something which is within reach and tangible upon its' revelation and upon our receiving of it.

A Declaration of Heaven is realizing that we have to teach our children the very nature of that which it is, that constitutes life, or why we choose as Parents and Adults to have children, and the joy and happiness that entails from such unconditional love and need of expression, which is to give, and to feel, and to know, and to learn, and to explore, and to understand, and to grow, but of all these pursuits, to also know what we are giving, and what we are feeling, and what to accept and acknowledge, and what are we learning, and where shall we explore, and what shall we understand, and how shall we grow within these pursuits, as we cannot idly expect that all is as it should be, unless we have permitted it to be so, as many of us, are already well rehearsed, and well planned, and well experienced in our everyday lives to somewhat predict what good fortunes or ill-fate may come our way, as we may have the understanding and ability to invite or dispel them at will, as we have witnessed and experienced such realties through our own constant ties to our families and friends and associates and colleague alike.

A Declaration of Heaven is to start living, and to start observing, and to start watching, and to start partaking in all the many wonders and activities of things that have shaped and influenced our lives, we must remember to take note, and to put down our thoughts of action into some form of coherent plan or strategy, so as to improve upon our current situation, as we must also fill our minds with the things that brings us fulfillment and joy and wonder, and invest in the things that we aspire to teach and to share with one another, as we must learn to enjoy and to celebrate our freedoms of liberation at every available chance, and we must be well aware that what we know who, and what we are in our realization and acceptance of one another, or at least who or what we are becoming in our everyday lives, so that we may live it, and we must remember that every day we must practice what we preach, as we share this life and this universe along with our families and friends, as the Moon does not care what will happen to us tomorrow, as the Moon has its own mastery and position within the heavens, and the Sun does not care what will happen to us, as the Sun has its' own responsibility within the heavens, but as sure as they are ever present in our lives, it is by knowing that it is through our associations and relationships with one another, that we should care what will happen to us tomorrow, and what will happen to our families and friends, as in our concerns, we have a care and duty to serve and fulfill as a lifelong loving obligation to be there for one another in the best and in the worst of times.

A Declaration of Heaven, is to influence one another in both a good and positive way, and to help each other improve and succeed in life, as this is the point in life, to try to aim to achieve to be better, so that we can appreciate all that life has to offer, as we cannot wait for life to simply pass us by, simply by wishing or believing that all would come to us by faith alone, as we must try, and we must do, and we must begin to try to get along, to get from somewhere so as to end up somewhere else in a positive place, as such is the journey from one point in time to another, that we are not made to be standing still, as we are made to keep pushing on in our learning, to keep journeying, and to keep discovering in order to gain our fulfillment of satisfaction.

A Declaration of Heaven is to open our minds, to the many possibilities that life has to offer, as we must allow each other to flourish, in the many varied and aspects of our teaching and learning, as we did when we were children at school, where the world and its' possibilities were larger than life, in a place where we had a variety of diverse subjects to choose to learn from and study, and so why is it that when we become Adults, that we no longer focus upon such inherent and interesting subjects, and yet as it is we seek to bury our heads in the sands of time, allowing pessimism and ignorance to take over, but why should we stop learning and engaging with these challenging ideas that we were once encouraged to take up as children, if only for us to then suddenly stop one day asking questions of things that we need to know, things that matter as we navigate ourselves from one place in time to another.

As it has always been said that a Mind is a terrible thing to waste, and yet here we are idly sitting by as the world seeks to go on without us, but no, this is your life, as much as it is mine, and as much as it is anyone else's life, and so we must wake up and shake up our minds, and take comfort, that each day is a new day to attempt to change, or to try to do something new or positively different or challenging within this new aspiration and dedication and expectation of life.

A Declaration of Heaven, as well as being a place where this imagination of enlightened knowledge brings us much closer together within our warmth and acceptance of each other, it is through our cooperation with one another, and also where there are less and less dividing lines to set us apart from one another, that we in maintaining a practical and suitable environment for ourselves, and one that sustains our moral and ethical well-being, and where we can commune within our social activity, and gravitate towards engaging and expressing our shared union, by commanding and exploring, through our language and words and skills, whilst constantly applying and upholding our Dignity and Respect in proportion with that which is deemed necessary for such a worthy cause, which in a fashion, is suited to both a formal and casual setting for us to find love, peace and harmony in proximity with one another.

A Declaration of Heaven, is not necessarily a question of whether we are Rich or Poor, but more a question of our perspective and outlook on life, as to whether we can uphold and deliver such a principled view, for such a declaration to take root and effect in the state of our minds, and in our lives, and that is to say that it is time to change the World before the World changes us, for we must accept, that for us to grow, then we need to change, and sometimes we need to change for us to grow, and so we must allow for changing and growth to be of a particular importance, to us and our future projections of acquiring or obtaining this uniformity of Heaven.

A Declaration of Heaven is for us to acquire, and to obtain such a Global unified standing, so as to be aware that what we wish and even desire to overcome, and well, to be basically better at, or more improved at, or more advanced at, is to be assured of the way within ourselves, and within this new sense of self-worth and maturity, which is by now being nurtured and developed inside of us, and so we must embrace it, along with this new sense of belonging to a greater construct which is the Word at large, as we must constantly learn to accept this Universal and integral and internal evolution of ourselves, as being both a unique and dynamic Human event, both inwardly and outwardly, taking shape and effect in our lives, and upon the nature of our spirit, and within the very nature of our personality and character.

A Declaration of Heaven is to find a panacea and a way to cement solutions towards our ever eventful landscape, which is upon reflection the World in which we all live and dwell within, and of course in knowing that we cannot cure every single advancing problem on such a massive and Global scale, even if we in ourselves were to mediate and believe it could truly be so, but in order to take affirmative action to do, and even if we are convinced enough in our determinations to believe that such is the greatest test and challenge in the trials of our lives, which is to attempt to do so, as in all reality and helplessness, it would only be a mere infantile, if not futile and idled gesture of dreaming, set against a backdrop of naivety and wishful thinking to believe so.

As the World is not purely shaped or driven by such ideologies of invention, as we in ourselves attempt to persist to comprehend all of its' Earthly richness and realistic endeavors with which for us to explore, as this also requires and commands a strategy and a much thought-out study and plan in the ideology of Man in its application, and granted in its' acceptance, that every good and workable idea may require some monetary backing, or investment and capital to become a practical and worthwhile venture of promise and satisfaction, except that not from the earthly riches of money, but from the milk of human kindness, comes the true allowances of concessions, provisions and incentives if only to yield and to warrant such a declaration that is fit for the purpose and the practice of living, as we have already established every optional resource open to us, and we also have every reason and purpose to believe that the World and the knowledge embedded and encoded in the History of our World may still yet yield us the benefits, that we are aiming to obtain, and that some, but not all possibilities are endless, but also that life on the whole in its' examination, is and has always been good for us, to begin to know, and to understand, that as we make footprints through this World, that this may still count for something, as being of an extraordinary value, and may be seen by future generations as something of worthiness, even before our fulfillment is infinitely complete.

A Declaration of Heaven, is for each and every one of us, to make a promise to ourselves, to be and to do whatever we can, and the best that we can do, is to be true and sincere to the virtue of helping one another, and to create and build such relationships, and to make a better and brighter World for ourselves, and however we may choose, or come by to try to attempt, or to interpret such a vision or reality, that we in turn would find amazement and wonder growing out from its' roots, in realizing and knowing that we could reach into the depths of the unknown, and somehow come out the other side having tried and succeeded, in going beyond the average, ordinary and mundane expectations of what our interpretation of Heaven on Earth, or Peace in the World should appear to be, or come to reflect upon in all of us potential visionaries, as this unknown future is yet to be lived and is still yet to be travelled and experienced by all of us who are seeking to make such promises as a daily practice in our lives, especially in the face of challenging adversity, even as we seek to grow, and to evolve, and to believe in knowing that what we can and must do to improve upon to become better, which in itself is to become a better reflection of one another in the World.

A Declaration of Heaven, is acknowledging that the future is what we can and must endeavor to progress towards, in maintaining and creating it as a whole, in what we can eventually one day proclaim it to be, not only for ourselves but also for the benefit of those who are about to be become born into this world, as we in ourselves have also rightly been prepared for that same reason, for we were already well prepared and established in our countless experiences that have led us from one to the other, and also away from the deprivations, and the disastrous consequences of our ill-fated decline into the depths of wrath, greed, envy, sloth, pride, lust, and gluttony, if only for us once again, to begin to rise to the challenge of seeking to ascent, and begin working towards our greater aspirations of Human nature, which is to achieve the qualities of prudence, justice, temperance, fortitude, faith, hope and charity, upon this lifelong journey toward a better view and purpose and practice of life in demonstrating what it truly means to be Human, and to move much more closer towards our naturally inherent values of good and positive intentions and behavior.

As we have proven to ourselves time and time again, that when we come together as a Family to address minuscule Family problems, that surely we can solve and address and put our minds and hearts together to make a difference, especially when it really matters to each and every person concerned, as even in our Family values when we often enough, we have to deal with problems or disputes, in that it is without reservation so as to achieve peace of mind and an understanding, that we should work through them as a unit of Family members, as we would naturally and automatically deal with them at source and squash them before they can take root or disrupt our invaluable Family ties, and so in this light, we must also extend this effort, and this philosophy of cooperation with one another, and extend it even further, into and with our Universal Worldly Family ties, and engage to work together, and work through what can often be both a challenging and difficult problem in order to begin to address and sort out our Worldly problems.

A Declaration of Heaven is to one day see that dreams come true, and wishes are granted, and promises are kept, and hope is fulfilled, and agreements are adhered to, and undoubtedly prayers are answered, as even the World wants to meet with itself upon the higher plains of wisdom and enlightenment, to celebrate its' own union and oneness of its' people, and the World wants to fall in love with itself and its' many cultures that live and dwell upon within its' furthest corners, and the World also wants to liberate itself in the name of a new found freedom of expression and independence for all its many people who have wondered and gazed up at the skies and the stars above, for we are the World, and all that we are, we shall always encompass within us as being the wonders of the World.

A Declaration of Heaven is to look in the mirror of illusion and reflection, and to see the Human form of our being, and to begin to realize that this is the representation of mankind and humanity in all of its' naturalness, as we are what we are regardless of where we come from, as this mirror of illusion and reflection can never lie to us, as it can only reveal to us the true form of ourselves, as if by definition, it need not speak or mention or utter any words of intention with which to define itself, as it need not question or interrogate itself, as it is what is, and it is also because we are what we are, as if by comparison, it need not have any real distinction of what it is in our being and form from one to the other.

A Declaration of Heaven is to look at this Human form and being, and be without judgment upon its' acceptable appearance, and so therefore how can it love or hate, and how can it be deceitful or honest, or how can it be right or wrong, as such are the imperfections of the world that it is placed within, and such are the perfections of that which the world has inside of its' being, coupled along with that which brings us to inquire after such questioning and examination of itself, so as to ask of ourselves, who could love or hate it, if not itself, and who could be deceitful or honest with it, if not itself, and how can it be right or wrong, if not to pass judgment upon it for it to be made acceptable upon the appearance of itself, and so we must find our initial inherent Human form of being, of firstly being that which is our first proclaimed uniformity and identity, which is that of our first and foremost acceptance and signature within the declaration of heaven.

Angelus Domini

INSPIRIT * ASPIRE * ESPRIT * INSPIRE

.ONE.XV.

~*~

Angelus Domini

A Tao. **House** Product
Angel Babies .ONE.
INSPIRIT*ASPIRE*ESPRIT*INSPIRE
Valentine Fountain of Love Ministry
Info contact: ***tao.house@live.co.uk***
Copyright: Clive Alando Taylor 2019

~*~

Printed in the United States
By Bookmasters